C000224486

the graduate alphabet

A
Adulthood
Accountability
Alright...so what next?
Anti-climax
Appearance
Approval
Armour
Ask

B
Banking
Bible Reading
Booze
Bosses

C
Car
Church
City Life
Committed
Cover Letters
Cuppa Tea
CVs

D
Dare
Detour
Diaries
Dinners
Direction
Doh!
Dreams

E
Emptiness
Expectancy

F
Facebook
Fear
Forget
Friendships
Fun

G
Generosity
Graduation
Guidance

H
Healthy Eating
Hector
Hidden
Hobbies
Holy
Honesty
House Sharing
Human

I
Identity
Independence
Interviews
Insomnia
Integrity
Intentionality
Isolation

J
Jobs

K
Kit Kat

L
Lounge
Love

M
Marriage
Mexican

N
Neglect
Neighbours
Newbie

O
Office Politics
Oliver
Ouch!

P
Pace
Parents (living away)
Parents (living with them)
Promotion
Puff
Purpose

Q
Quiz

R
Redundancy
Responsible
Rest
Ross Kemp

S
Sex
Shifts
Singleness
Small Fish, Big Pond
Stuck
Student Loans
Success

T
Tube Pass
Transparent

U
Umbrella

V
Vanilla

W
West Ham
Work Experience

X
Xena Warrior Princess

Y
Year Out
Youth

Z
Zero

Liz Clark is a dancer and a mum to two very boisterous boys. She works freelance for organisations across the East Midlands and has a passion for supporting families. She regularly leads creative movement sessions for pre-school children and children on the autistic spectrum or with profound and multiple disabilities. Have a look at her stuff at www.lizclark.net. When she's not dancing she enjoys sleeping, Haribo and watching period dramas.

George Critchley lives and works in Sheffield, where he is a Creative Campaigns Manager for a marketing agency. He and his wife are part of St Thomas' Church Philadelphia, where he co-leads a missional community. He loves to explore the messages of modern culture and their relationship with the message of Jesus. He enjoys writing poetry and short plays, cooking to the sound of Ray Charles, and great cinema. His favourite crisps are Tyrrell's Sweet Chilli and Red Pepper.

James Featherby has worked in the City for over 30 years, mostly as a corporate partner of one of the world's leading law firms. He studied theology and law at Cambridge. He has written two books on reforming business, started numerous Christian projects in the City, and invests in social impact businesses in the UK and Africa. He advises the Church of England on ethical investment.

Alexander Lee is a 28-year-old journalist and author. He wrote the #pray4 principle that explored the prayer campaign behind the incredible recovery of footballer Fabrice Muamba. Alexander lives in York, loves sport and is a local football manager. He eats too much protein. Follow Alexander on twitter @randomalexander.

Sarah-Jane Marshall works for LICC in the Work Forum team, where she's heading up a new project seeking to equip 18-30s to see how God can work in and through them in their daily work. She studied Art History at York University and has since worked for an MP and two charities. She lives and worships in South London with her husband Joe where they enjoy hosting lively dinner parties.

Anna Mathur is a Student and Women's Pastor at St Mark's in Battersea. With a heart for women and young adults, she loves getting stuck into life issues and seeing people seeking and stepping into the Freedom that Jesus has for them. Anna also works as a Psychotherapist for the NHS and enjoys writing and baking in her spare time.

All Change

Transitions are times of change. For graduates, the transition from university life into the adult working world is one that often involves change on multiple levels. New job? New finances? New location? New church? New friends? New relationship status? New role in the world?

So much change all at once can be overwhelming.

It's quite normal to feel 'all at sea' in this new season, especially when some changes might be things we wouldn't choose for ourselves: 'I didn't expect to be doing a job like this, but it's all I can find for now' or 'I didn't expect to be forced to move back in with my parents until I found a job'.

But change is only the context; it doesn't have to set the tone.

From beginning to end the Bible speaks of the unchanging nature of God – he is a firm rock, a King of the Ages, one from everlasting to everlasting. We trust in the eternal, covenant God who doesn't waiver on his promises.

And in this new chapter of life, the principles of Christian living stay the same too. Our financial situation may change, but we're still called to be a people that trust in God's provision and live generously. Similarly, we may now be doing paid work instead of academic work, but we're still called to steward our talents and work 'as if working for the Lord'.

In the following entries, you will find wisdom from a range of voices. Some are recent grads themselves, others have seen a bit more of life, but all have insights into the challenges and opportunities of life after uni.

I hope this collection will encourage you, inspire you and remind you that although your context is changing, the opportunity to live life with and for Jesus stays the same.

Sarah-Jane Marshall

'Be strong and courageous. Do not be afraid; do not be discouraged, for the LORD your God will be with you wherever you go.'
- Joshua 1:9

Adulthood - Sarah-Jane

CONGRATULATIONS! YOU MADE IT THROUGH UNIVERSITY!

So are you a big, fully-fledged adult now? Even three years after graduating, there are lots of days when I don't really feel like an adult. I still have a childlike sense of achievement when I complete a train journey that has more than one interchange. And I still find the sight of pigeons trying to mate hilarious, even if I am watching from my very grown-up office desk!

Our culture tells us that 'adulthood' is something horribly boring and serious that, like Peter Pan, we should try to hold at bay for as long as possible. But the reality is that you're already an adult! You don't have to wait until you are married or a home-owner to 'settle down' and enter adulthood – this new stage of life begins now.

Words like 'mature' and 'responsible' don't only have to have negative connotations – they also signal the opportunity to step out in new ways with God in the world and to use your gifts and abilities to serve society. Some people will tell you that your university years are the 'best years of your life'. For me, they were wonderful years and it's true, I'll never have years quite like them again. But don't worry, this is by no means the end of the story – this new chapter has plenty more exciting things to be grabbed with both hands!

And mating pigeons will always be funny.

Accountability - George

Accountability and support from a close friend are crucial at this stage in life. In a new place, with a new routine, where you can be tempted to look for comfort in unhealthy things, it's important to have someone connected to you who knows your weaknesses: maybe bad eating habits, self-esteem issues, the websites you're prone to visit or self-destructive patterns that you can't help yourself out of.

My advice would be to arrange accountability with a long-standing friend for at least the first six months after uni and then work on finding someone closer, perhaps from your (new?) church. Having that same person looking out for you, as you will for them, is really valuable. It also means that you feel supported, which is especially precious in situations where you might come home after a long day at work and have no-one to chat to about your day, your week and the challenges you're facing.

"Have at least one person you can meet with regularly for coffee – this has been a lifeline for me in the busy periods where I've struggled to make it to church." - Chloe, 27

Alright... so, what next? - George

You've been promising yourself that by this point you'd have a plan. But maybe time got away from you. Or plan-making was too daunting, and became replaced by more pressing concerns, ranging from the sub-plots in One Tree Hill and House, to more genuine concerns, like final exams, coursework and cherishing time with friends.

Either way, you've graduated. And you might have a plan, but aren't sure how to feel about it, or the plan doesn't exist. Time to panic, right?

Not really. One thing to remember is that a lot of other people are in your position. Another thing to remember is that a gap year won't solve it all. Unfortunately, your detailed plan of action probably won't come to you in the middle of a rainforest in Borneo.

In a sense, if you lack an immediate trajectory this can be a blessing in disguise. While the momentum created by travel through decades of education can be helpful, it can also blind you from the need for you to generate your own momentum. Instead of ending up where your gifts/parents/employers take you, it's better to assess the landscape, decide where you want to be, and walk there. This is all part of being intentional, something you'll bump into later on (in the 'I' section).

Having no plan means that you get to write one with God. Let him excite your imagination; let him remind you of the gifts he gave you. But don't expect to get a five-point plan of how you will get where you want to be. Concentrate on the step ahead, the intermediate goal and pursue that.

The Israelites in the desert followed God's leading pillar of fire on a day-by-day basis. They had guidance and sufficient food for each day. And if he moved, they moved.

Get ready for an adventure with God. Then just start walking.

"For the first time in my life, I didn't have something lined up to go back to in September. So many years of naturally progressing to the next educational step and now I faced what seemed like a huge cliff-edge. The uncertainty was terrifying. It really forced me to push into God in prayer."
- Nic, 26

"The out-working of God's calling might look very different at different stages of your life and that's OK! The challenge is to seek God's will for the present and ask for your 'daily bread' - God's provision for today."
- Josh, 22

Anti-climax - Sarah-Jane

I don't know about you, but I grew up thinking I was going to change the world. I was going to do really well at school and university and then go out and do the stuff with a bang.

It wasn't just a naïve, overly confident hope either, but something that people spoke over me, prayed for me and sang alongside me. I was going to be part of the 'history making' generation that really changed the world for Jesus.

Then my first job mostly involved opening someone else's mail and drafting standardised letters in response. Not glamorous, not world-shattering, but serving someone in a position of office in the everyday tasks of working life.

Not many graduates will parachute straight into high-flying jobs. In fact, even those fortunate enough to get places on sought-after grad schemes will probably spend the first few years doing quite menial tasks as they complete their training. So does that mean that as recent graduates we can't 'do the stuff', that we can't 'change the world' yet?

The tension centres on what our idea of 'changing the world' is. Can it be on a huge scale, affecting hundreds or thousands of people? Maybe, for some people. James Davison Hunter in his ironically titled book, 'To Change the World' says that actually our aim should be to practise 'faithful presence' - to be a fragrant community that models Christ in all of our relationships and our everyday work in every sphere of life.

Whatever you do, whether it is shiny and impressive, or actually quite ordinary, you can serve Jesus. This idea is so important that we are going to come back to it in several other chapters ('Dare', 'Dreams', 'Emptiness', 'Hidden', 'Holy', 'Integrity', 'Purpose' and 'Success').

"Be willing to do the tasks that are more mundane, do them diligently and to the best of your ability, and in time you'll be trusted with more challenging and stretching work. The Lord will humble you in this season, but remember that all things work for the good of those he loves." - Heather, 24

"I'm often tempted to believe that my Christian influence isn't all that great because I'm not seeing the radical kind of change achieved by biblical characters. I have to remind myself that God works in the everyday things too. Right now perhaps he is just as interested in how I manage my team as the big policy changes that we might be able to achieve." - Jonathan, 27

Appearance - Alexander

If there's one thing you need to prepare for whilst enjoying the back end of your university experience, it's a change of dress sense. For weeks I refused to come to terms with the fact that when I entered the post-university realm I had to consider shelving my baggy jeans, bright yellow t-shirts and torn flip-flops. How I longed for a world where you wear whatever you want in the office and only be judged on how hard you worked!

Unfortunately, have a dress code is a social convention that isn't going anywhere anytime soon. So, like me, you could fight the imminent dress code shift, or you could have a sense of humour about it and see it as a way of demonstrating to your employer that you are on board with them. Get yourself a budget (maybe ask one of your parents to loan you £100), pick a close friend, and head to the high street. Try to spend wisely. Look for bargains. Get two or three outfits for work. For all you lads try to pick good shirt and tie combos.

When you turn up for the first day of work, dress the part. It'll give those around you confidence in your ability and it will probably boost your own confidence too

Approval - James

We all respond well to praise. From our first tentative steps as a toddler to our faltering attempts at reading our first words, it's the excited 'well done' that spurs us on to try even harder. And, by and large, as you've continued to develop through the education system your parents, peers, teachers and tutors will have let you know when you've done well.

You'll notice a bit of a change once you start work. Rather than commending you for a job well done, your boss is likely to be too busy to notice or even care. At college you'll get a First for the 70% you do well; at work it's the 30% that's not quite up to scratch that gets highlighted.

While we all need approval and a bit of reassuring praise every now and then, it can be hard to come by in the workplace. For many, work is, quite literally, a thankless task. You've earned your wage, what more do you want?

The good news is you have a 100% approval rating from God. He loves you unconditionally. With that in your back pocket, the approval of your boss is always secondary. You are who God says you are. Believe it and seek to please him first.

"To God, you're already a success through
Jesus, with or without your career." - Bex, 24

Armour - George

A great spiritual habit to develop each day before leaving the house is to put on the armour of God (Ephesians 6:10-20).

It may feel a little unnecessary, but don't be deceived into thinking that what you do in your workplace doesn't have any eternal consequences. So stand in the front of the mirror (clothed or not, each to their own eh?) and put on:

+ The Belt of Truth.

+ The Breastplate of Righteousness.

+ Running Shoes with the Readiness that come from Powerful Good News that brings Peace.

+ The Shield of Faith.

+ The Helmet of Salvation.

+ The Sword at your side of God's Word, made sharp by the Holy Spirit.

If you remind yourself of these beauties before you head off on the commute, you'll be surprised how focused you are when you get to work.

N.B. Please remember to actually get dressed as well, or you might end up not having a job to commute to...

Ask - Alexander

Though there is a general perception that students and graduates are as welcome in the adult world as pigeons in a swimming pool...fear not. Asking for help from older people is imperative in the office or the dole queue. Ask someone more experienced for careers advice, about how to write a cover letter and what to ask at interview. You never know, asking for help could be the beginning of a valuable long-lasting friendship.

However, keep a wise hat on when doing this. Women, make sure the man you approach knows you're not flirting. Men, make sure the women you approach knows you don't have ulterior motives.

"My first job was extremely busy and a pretty steep learning curve. It was good to remember that I was just starting and therefore couldn't know everything or be as good as those more established than I. Ask for help and advice from God and those around you both at home and at work." – Caz, 27

Banking - Anna

So now you've left university, you can say, 'Goodbye to debt. Goodbye overdraft!' Never again will you have to dodge the 'balance' button on the cash machine. Chance would be a fine thing! If you have managed to leave University with no debt – that's fantastic! But do keep reading because I have a few tried and tested ideas up my sleeve.

When it comes to debt, the Bible actually likens it to slavery. Proverbs 22:7 says 'The rich rules over the poor, and the borrower becomes the lender's slave.' Some of us genuinely feel that way, we feel enslaved by our debt. Some of who have become 'used to' and apathetic about our debt perhaps should feel more enslaved!

These seven B's will help:

1: Book... an appointment with your bank and chat through the options available to you. Make sure you know how much interest you are paying and take time to shop around! Some banks offer graduate overdrafts which stagger the amount you pay interest on.

2: Budget... That word fills many with dread. But it's a great way of seeing where your pennies are going. We are, after all, stewards of our money – so knowing exactly where it goes can actually be quite freeing! Create a simple Excel spreadsheet, or download a budget app.

3: Be down with the lingo... You know that overdraft you have? The one that seduced you with promises of free rail cards and cinema tickets? Pretty soon, the student perk of 'Interest Free' will be a vague memory. Be savvy. Know your bank. Know what they offer you; swot up on interest rates and overdraft fees. Learn the financial jargon.

4: Buy with hard cash... If only you knew how liberating this has been for me! I will forever wave the flag for living in cash! We take out a particular amount each week for everything – food, toiletries, dry cleaning and socialising. And once it's gone, it's gone. It can be hard work – but nothing beats the feeling of knowing where your money is.

5: Branch out... Enrol on your local Christians Against Poverty (CAP) course. Log on to www.capmoney.org to find one near you. CAP run a three-week course on budgeting that helps you get a handle on your finances.

6: Be Courageous... If you are in debt, face it head on. It won't go away, it will only get bigger. Talk to your bank and work out a payment plan – don't live in fear. Don't fall for the sales ploys of companies who promise to 'consolidate your debt' into one lump sum. Instead, research and investigate your options. You may be able to jiggle the money about a bit so that you are paying lower interest rates for the larger sums.

7: Bottom Line... Don't pay with tomorrow's money, or you'll end up enslaved to yesterday's bills.

Bible Reading - George

Ah, Bible reading! Once-a-day, twice-a-day, weekly, monthly, quarterly....?

If you've been a student, you've probably experimented with different ways of doing quiet time. Reading God's word once a day can have a life-changing effect on people and if you got into the routine of doing it and can keep it up when you work, that's great.

If, however, your routine has been thrown into disarray by bus/train timetables, and you don't find time to read the word every day, then don't worry. Prioritise finding a routine that works, that's sustainable and don't assume that reading the Bible is something you need to do alone. For centuries, Bible reading was a communal pursuit, as communities had to club together to afford one copy. So read it with a friend if it's easier, but whatever you do, however regular: keep reading.

David likens the word of God to a lamp for his feet and a light for his path (Psalm 119:105). The word of God comforts in the dark parts of life. The word of God illuminates truth and banishes the lies we are tempted to believe about ourselves. The word of God offers vital direction and instruction for the journey. It's God speaking to you. Keep reading. Keep listening.

"Working life is often so much more structured than student life, so structure your devotional time with God into your new routine from the start." - Anna, 26

"Try reading your Bible on the commute. It can help you to see the connection between what you are reading and the day ahead, and might even provoke a great conversation with the person you are sat next to!" - Antony, 29

Booze - Alexander

"Another drink mate?"

"Yeah go on, I'm in fulltime work now. My liver is probably a lot stronger as a result of my job. That's how it works isn't it? As soon as I get paid a salary my whole DNA changes and having more than four drinks is now completely fine. Hallelujah!"

Unfortunately, getting smashed after Friday's shift is hugely common in British working culture. You need to be serious about knowing your own limits. If you know you will lose control, it may be best to stay away completely. You might lose your street cred in the office by turning down the offer to hit the bars at the end of the week. And yes, this will be very hard at the time. And yes, your colleagues will rip it out of you for being a 'lightweight'. However, God knows how tempting it is to compromise your reputation, conviction and ultimately your faith. For Jesus himself was tempted in EVERY way.

So 'set your stall out early doors' – show you are determined to live differently. Better to be seen as a bit of a lightweight than risk losing self-control with those you'll be spending every working day with.

"As my work in the City is quite stressful and often involves very long hours, there's quite a culture of going for drinks to unwind. The culture's so strong; it's a challenge not to get carried away." – Ben, 28

Bosses - Anna

Unless you're self-employed, no matter what rung of the ladder you are on – you'll find yourself under the authority of a 'boss'. You might form a great relationship, one of mutual respect and even friendship. But on the other hand, it may be a little more difficult.

In 1 Timothy 6:1, Paul tells us that 'all under the yoke of slavery should consider their masters worthy of full respect, so that God's name and our teaching may not be slandered'.

If slaves are to respect their masters, surely I should respect my boss. But what I find even more challenging is that Paul doesn't say, 'If they are good, if they deserve respect, if you like them – then respect them.' We are to give respect regardless.

You may find times in your working life that this is an easy ask. It's easy to respect someone who deserves it. At other times it may be a struggle – not everyone is likeable. So what do you do then? How do you respect someone who is unreasonable, criticising or unfair. Prayerfully! Don't attempt to do it in your own strength, instead pray for perseverance, patience, wisdom and whatever else you may need to honour God in respecting your boss. Prayer is powerful, prayer changes and redeems. It might be that you see changes in your boss, but you are more likely to find that the person who changes most is you.

If you are struggling with the relationship with your boss, ask God to help you see him through his eyes.

Car - Alexander

For those of you who work in the same city or town in which you live, why not consider leaving your car at home? This might mean you waking up ten or fifteen minutes earlier than usual, but it'll be worth it. Whether you walk or cycle to work, your heart and lungs will be thankful. The number of graduates who pack on the pounds soon after starting work is incredible.

Though you may think university life is the most tiring thing in the world, trust me, tiredness is relative. When you finish your first week at work you'll be crawling into your bed. The thought of exercise will be about as appealing as a tarmac-toastie. However, fifteen minutes of walking or cycling to and from work will help keep the weight off. (Even better, join a gym or a local sports team.)

Church - Liz

You may find yourself moving church community due to a change in study centre or a new job. Don't expect churches in other places to be exactly like your university church; as a church is made up of its members, you will never be able to recreate the same community and that's OK. Look for a church where Jesus is at the heart of the community. Look for Jesus in people, you'll find him. You can discover and celebrate Jesus in people whatever age they are.

When choosing a church, be careful not to judge churches against each other. It's important to find somewhere that will be good for you at this time, but churches are not consumer products to 'shop around' for according to how best they meet your needs. A church is a community where you should expect to give of yourself and serve others as much as you receive.

Don't worry if you can't find one immediately, but don't spend six months floating between churches, else you will struggle to put down strong roots. In a time of change, finding a strong church family will be key to keeping close to God.

"I found it quite hard letting go of my status as a 'student' in church. There was no longer a dedicated ministry for me and I had to be much more active seeking help and support when I needed it." – Amy, 26

"Be proactive! Get stuck into a local church as soon as you've settled on one – put yourself out there and try to build relationships as quickly as you can. It might feel a bit awkward at first, but will soon pay off." – Adam, 24

City Life - George

City life can easily be described as an oxymoron.

When lots of people live close to each other, they tend to act more selfishly. In one sense, it's understandable. Initiating and maintaining a meaningful relationship with every person you encounter is only a possibility in a small community like a village or a university college. In a city, trying to do the same would be emotionally exhausting and completely unsustainable.

As a protection mechanism, people tend to build a lovely wall around themselves and if they can control what occurs within that bubble, they absolutely will. Identity becomes a strange thing, because the sheer scale of the tapestry of humanity encountered in a big city can feel like it smothers or renders meaningless any individual uniqueness.

Responses to this can be to try to declare identity by dressing or acting a certain way. Or, it can lead to a numbness and lack of identity, meaning you cling to whatever defining characteristics are offered at the time – Mac/PC, Labour/Tory, X-Factor/ Strictly etc. Your identity comes from your relationship with God, the more you realise this, the more your peace will be recognisable to you and others.

Here's a challenge for people who live in the city. Remind yourself daily of the precious image of God that lies in every person you encounter on your commute. Embrace the unpredictable and spontaneous; be willing to start a conversation on the train if God prompts you. Preserve the beauty of relationship – it's what God made us for.

Committed - James

The working world is becoming increasingly competitive. To do well, you will have to work harder than you've ever worked before. And the higher you rise, the greater the demands on your time. Time will become more precious. Protect it. Prioritise it. Be clear about the things that matter most.

Make time for friends, particularly your Christian friends – those people who support, encourage and love you, no matter what. And, as the writer to the Hebrews says: 'Let us not give up meeting together, as some are in the habit of doing'. Your church family is what will sustain you. They keep you grounded and accountable; they keep you focused on the true goal of your life. Give up meeting together and your career may well thrive in the short-term, but your faith will wither in the long-term.

Cover Letters - Anna

That annoying page that partners your CV. More important than we think – some companies get hundreds of CVs a week and it's the cover letter that will set you apart.

Here are a few handy tips:

+ Ensure the reader doesn't feel like their company is just another on your list (even if it is). Make it clear as to why you're applying.

+ Always address the letter to a specific person. You might have to do a bit of detective work, but it'll be worth it.

+ Your cover letter should reflect the industry you are applying to. If it is a design agency for example, why not add a splash of colour?

+ Name drop! Why not! If you have had some great work experience, or worked on a particular project or for a well-known client – make it known.

+ Inject your personality into it somehow, perhaps make it a little conversational.

+ Ensure you proofread your CV and cover letter thoroughly, mistakes will often find your letter in the 'no' pile, no matter how wonderful the content.

Then why not pray whilst sending them off? Pray that they fall into the right hands, pray for the people reading them. Pray that the right door may be opened – and a harder prayer – that the wrong doors may be shut fast.

Cuppa Tea? - Anna

Someone once said, 'Tea is liquid wisdom.' Now I wouldn't quite agree, but what I do believe is that the simple act of making people tea can change things.

If you want to get a glimpse of an office environment – look at how they make tea! My office now is very communal with a real family feel. Cakes are often baked and shared, sweets bought and huge rounds of tea made.

However, I once worked in an every-man-for-himself office. Or, as I liked to call it – a 'tea-for-one office'. In I swept – doing big office rounds, adhering to people's odd tea habits (four sugars and the teabag left in – yuck!) and baking communal treats. Initially people questioned my kindness: who is this new girl and what does she want?

But it didn't take long before things changed. People began making drinks for one another and I even came back to my desk to the odd chocolate bar! What a change! And all because of a few cups of tea.

So, when you start your new job. Put down your bag, say 'Hi' and get the kettle on!

"In my first job I offered to wash someone's mug and they were literally speechless as that just wasn't done. It's the small things."
– Jo, 30

CVs - Anna

Your CV is your interview ticket. It's what you will be judged on before you even darken the doorstep of a potential employer. Sometimes employers will have their own application form which will include all your key information, whereas others will ask for a separate CV.

In either case, you need to be vigilant on structure and a little OCD about your spelling. I have worked for employers who admit that even if they spot one little spelling mistake – it goes straight in the bin. It sounds a little drastic right? But when your inbox or mail tray is full of CVs you can understand why they set the bar so high. Get a few friends to check it over for you as they will probably spot things that you don't.

The ideal CV is only one page of A4 in length, so find creative ways (without reducing everything to teensy-weensy size 8 font!) to get all your vital information on without being too wordy.

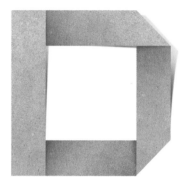

Dare - Anna

The term 'I dare you' used to get batted around the school playground as we encouraged each other to push boundaries and stretch limits.

But I like to think that now it is God ushering us to step out, daring us to believe and live what he has for our lives. Daring us to push earthly boundaries and assumed limits. He dares us to believe that he is a God of the now, that he is a God of miracles and redemption. It's as if he is saying, "Do you believe that you, little you, can be a huge part of that? You can be my hands, my feet. You can see miracles, lives changed, people saved."

When a man pleaded with Jesus to heal his son he cried out, "Lord I believe, but help my unbelief" (Mark 9:24). This may be your prayer – 'God I believe you are who you say you are, but help the doubting part of me. Help me walk forward into a life saturated by you. Help me have courage to dare to step out into all you have for me as your child, so that I might see you work in my life and those around me – for your glory.'

So there's the challenge. Do you dare to accept it, to pray it, to live it? Dreaming is one thing, taking the courage to make the steps to see it happen is another.

"I struggled on the first day with feeling inadequate. I prayed though my role and asked God to do it through me. That put the role in perspective – I am not in this alone. Remembering this removed the pressure of performance from the job and freed me to enjoy working hard and loving the people around me, knowing that he would use my efforts." – Jordan, 23

Detour - Alexander

Explore! If you are moving to a new town, city or planet, make sure you explore the alleyways and avenues. Don't just know the route to church/work/mate's house – but get to know the heart of where you live.

The feeling of being lost is awful for a child. It's often worse for an adult. Whether you buy, download or draw yourself a map, remember you need to know where you are eventually. Ask someone at your new church to give you the tour of the town. Make notes of good pubs, restaurants and theatres. Give yourself loads of things to look forward to.

Even though you might not feel like an adult, pretending to be one is a great laugh. You might even want to push the boat out and become a member of a local society or club. Before you know it you'll be chatting about protected birds, local footballers and art installations with your new friends Derek and Martha. Happy days.

Diaries - Anna

Why own a diary when the extent of your organisation is ringing up a mate and letting them know you'll be round in five (that is – if they have any food in the fridge)?

Maybe your life was jam packed with meetings and tutorials, or perhaps it was more rhythmic and predictable. Whether diaries lay gathering dust, or were filled to the brim, you will find them particularly useful in the working world.

Psychological research concludes that our short-term memory can hold on average seven pieces of information! That won't get us very far! I diarise everything, from coffees with friends to payment dates. As soon as a date gets thrown around – it goes in!

It can help schedule, prioritise, chronicle, journal and mark achievements. But most importantly, it has saved me from double booking, getting lost (I tend to jot down post codes too) and being late.... most of the time.

So, make good friends with your iCal, Google planner, iPhone calendar or a good old-fashioned paper diary. And...download a handy birthday app so you'll never be in trouble with your Mum for forgetting her birthday!

Dinners - Anna

Who sits at your dinner table? Housemates? Family? Or perhaps you scoff your meal down before rushing out, or prefer to munch in front of the television?

In Middle Eastern culture, eating together was so important and the act of sharing a meal indicated equality. Jesus challenged people's perceptions of who should share in this intimate activity by eating with people from all walks of life. You can imagine that the Pharisees were outraged!

However, those close to Jesus saw the power and love in his decision to eat with sinners and followed his lead. In Matthew 9:10, 'Matthew invited Jesus and his disciples to his home as dinner guests, along with many tax collectors and other disreputable sinners'.

So, how can we as disciples of Jesus follow his lead? Who are our equivalent of 'tax collectors' that we can invite to eat around our table? Why not rustle up a good British Sunday roast and invite the tough old lady next door, or the troubled friend-of-a-friend? You'll probably see people change as they are challenged by the inclusive kindness you show.

Ask God today if there is someone he'd like you to invite round for pizza.

"Have patience. Don't feel like the first job or first type of work is where you have to stay for the rest of your life. It's an experience you can use to build on." - Dave, 30

"If you have had to take 'any old job' just to keep a roof over your head, be sure also to remember your dream career. Don't lose yourself." - Josie, 29

Direction - Liz

It's OK not to know where you want to be. It might feel like all of your friends have 'a plan' and a clear idea of where they are heading, but they'll have days when they doubt their choices too.

The end goal might just be to live as God wants you to in your workplace. The Bible gives us far more direction about how we should work than where we should work. Similarly, there is far more on what kind of husband or wife you should be than who exactly you should marry.

Both my husband and I have done our fair share of moaning about our first few jobs, but there's no way we would be where we are now without those experiences and that training. It's so much easier to see God's hand in retrospect, so in the moment it's about learning to trust that he holds you tight.

Try not to be too intense about your direction. Waiting for 'signs' about every decision you make eventually becomes crippling. The right thing will unfold; you don't need a dramatic vision from God. He has set the boundaries in the Bible – read it, pray and use the wisdom he has given you to make your decisions with confidence.

Doh! - James

Pretty much every success story is littered with previous failures. For example, to be a really successful entrepreneur, it's almost a rite of passage to have built at least one business that has gone bust along the way. There's a reason for that; it's our mistakes that teach us the most.

If you begin your working life thinking you're the main event, you will soon learn you are not. And, more often than not, the lesson will involve you falling from a great height. But don't despair. However painful, embrace it, learn from it and move on.

"It takes courage to be prepared to say sorry when you are wrong at work, but it is ultimately releasing – don't hold back."
– Ruby, 22

"Learn how to take constructive criticism – when someone says, "That was stupid" it's not the same as them saying, "You are stupid". – Esther, 29

Dreams - Liz

When you're at university, it can feel like the world is your oyster – that you can do anything. Whatever dreams you might have had, the job or next situation you find yourself in might not feel like an outworking of your dreams. But, a word of encouragement, every step you take can be a step towards fulfilling those dreams.

Nothing is wasted. Be aware of where you are; any experience can be used to further your dream. Don't lose sight of where you want to get to, but instead keep offering your hopes and dreams to God in prayer. The more we lean into God, the more our dreams are likely to align with his will.

"Have patience. Don't feel like the first job or first type of work is where you have to stay for the rest of your life. It's an experience you can use to build on." – Dave, 30

"If you have had to take 'any old job' just to keep a roof over your head, be sure also to remember your dream career. Don't lose yourself." – Josie, 29

Emptiness - Alexander

For the majority of those who I have interviewed regarding leaving university, there often comes a sense of emptiness post-academia. It's often hard to put a finger on, but it can sometimes feel like a form of depression or grief. Though there's not a lot that can heal this temporary sensation, knowing that it is totally normal does help.

Vocalise what actually hurts. Speak to God, family members, friends, even pets. Whatever you do, don't quit. There are cases of graduates leaving their new job to move back home due to the overwhelming feeling of nostalgia. The truth is that the 'university you' is dead... long live the new you! You swam the river and enjoyed it thoroughly, but welcome to the ocean. The waves are bigger, the water is colder, but believe me it can be even more rewarding.

"Don't be ashamed to admit if you're struggling – it's a difficult time! Learn to talk about how you are feeling – you'll be surprised how many others are probably finding it hard too." – James, 25

"Be honest with your friends and family from the start when they ask how you are getting on. I found it harder to admit I was slipping once I really started slipping, so it would have been better to be honest from the outset." – Sara, 24

Expectancy - James

Don't be a wimp; exercise some spiritual muscle. Too many Christians have a survival mentality when they get to work. Instead, hold your head up. Have some faith. Decide to make a difference and relish the challenge. Expect the unexpected. That said, be aware of the context you find yourself in. Be inclusive. Be sensitive. Be wise.

Be deliberate and purposeful about the way you operate at work; be open to the transformative power of the values you live by and the God who accompanies you. You may be pleasantly surprised by the results. Expect God to be at work.

"Remember that the workplace is a place to worship God, not just somewhere to witness or buckle down the hatches and 'survive' as a Christian." - David, 25

"When I learnt to pray for my work, God showed me that my work didn't have to be just a mundane routine. You can turn any workplace into your mission field - it doesn't have to be dull!" - Anna, 23

Facebook - Anna

Love it or hate it, Facebook is a huge part of our social culture. I could reel out statistics that show how we have never been so well connected with the world and yet also so deeply disconnected from one another. But instead I want to challenge our use of Facebook.

We have never been so public. The more we use Facebook, the more of an expression of ourselves it can become. We 'update' thoughts, cringe over photos of parties gone by and browse through friends' profiles. We get a feel of a person by what they choose to portray publicly.

So, maybe we should look at our profiles from an outsider's perspective. If a stranger browsed your profile (let's hope your security settings are better than that – but just imagine for a moment), what picture would they build of you?

We are called to be in the world, but not of the world. So pictures of a night out with the girls/lads are fine – but risqué dress choices and snaps of drunken kisses really aren't. So if you find yourself dreading the appearance of last night's photos, alarm bells should be going off as to your behaviour!

I'm not saying that we should be sharing Bible verses every day and covering our pages in God apps, but perhaps we should second guess what we say, how we comment – and whether that dodgy looking photo, although honestly innocent, might give the wrong impression. If we are ambassadors of Jesus, maybe our profiles should reflect this too.

Ask yourself: What does your Facebook page say about you?

Fear - James

Starting work can be a scary prospect. However confident you are in your ability, if you don't have a few nerves on your first day, you probably aren't taking it seriously enough. But, beyond the surface worries about the newness of it all — meeting new people, operating unfamiliar equipment, wondering where the toilet is — we all carry deep-seated insecurities. We need to keep those insecurities in check because they do have the potential to haunt us throughout our careers.

For some, insecurities cause them to hide away; in many, they are a cause of a perpetual drive for 'success'. Part of the maturing process is becoming self-aware, recognising our 'drivers' and learning to override them when we need to. If you don't, they will, sooner or later, lead you astray.

And don't think it's only the 'weak' and 'feeble' who carry insecurities. Some of the coolest, most confident people you'll come across will have them by the bucket-load. If they tell you they don't, they're telling porkies!

Remember, love and fear can't co-exist. 1 John 4:16-18 says,

'And so we know and rely on the love God has for us. God is love. Whoever lives in love lives in God, and God in them. This is how love is made complete among us so that we will have confidence on the day of judgment: in this world we are like Jesus. There is no fear in love. But perfect love drives out fear, because fear has to do with punishment. The one who fears is not made perfect in love.'

Remain centered in Christ, secure in his love, and you will learn to conquer your insecurities.

Forget - Alexander

We long for what we used to know. During the initial stages of full-time work, we will naturally reminisce about our university days through brand new rose-tinted glasses. However, don't throw away your common sense.

It's normal and natural to think about what our fellow graduates are up to. It's normal and natural to send an occasional text or email.

It's not wise to try to recapture missed chances by chasing an old flame you rejected during university. Don't run after what you thought wasn't worth chasing in the first place.

"End well at uni. Make a definite end and try to be realistic about who you will keep in touch with and how often you will visit. Don't try to hold onto the old over embracing the new. Be grateful for what has been and be excited for what's ahead, recognising that it will be different." - Kat, 22

Friendships - George

The biggest challenge you will come up against in the first few years after leaving university for work, is the change in friendships.

It is the thing you notice first, mourn the longest and feel the hardest.

Think about your university friends. People you would call friends for life. Who you want at your bedside when ill, at hand during a crisis, the first people you think of to ring when you see or hear something amazing.

Now think about how far, in terms of distance and time those people were. One of them may have lived in the same house as you. Another might be a five minute walk away.

When you start work, these 'golden friends' are no longer all to hand. The contrast, between them being so immediately available and being in a different city or county, is huge.

My secret fantasy is to have all my 'golden friends' living together in a commune in a little secluded part of the world, but after long consideration, that tempting idea isn't realistic or necessarily godly: we can't stay together forever. We can keep in touch, but those aspects of their character that make them incredible friends should now be shared with the rest of the world.

A side note at this point would be to say this: don't compare new friendships that you make as a working person to the ones you've made during uni. It will dwarf them in comparison; it could kill them before they've grown. The contexts in which the two friendships grow are so different, uni friendships have so much more time and shared experience to build on.

Now this may sound a little pedestrian, but in the new place you go, where your friends aren't immediately around you, God is there. He is with you. When you start your new job, make him your first port of call for friendship and support, rather than making him second best. When your friend doesn't pick up the phone, he's there, available and ready to love you. And he knows you better than any of your friends, however 'golden' they are. Get used to going to him first.

Fun - Liz

Student life can be a very playful time and when you leave it's easy to feel, and therefore become, very serious. Make space in your leisure time for the fun things you love. Keep your sense of humour at work. Don't forget the fun.

Generosity - George

The best and worst thing about working is getting paid. Or more specifically, getting paid money. It's a tricksy little chap, whether in your bank or in your hand.

Whatever salary you're on, it's never enough. There are the student loans to pay back. Oh, and the overdraft to clear. And then there's the money you borrowed from your dad, a deposit on the flat, the first three months' rent upfront...It soon goes and it only gets worse the older you get, when mortgages and a family to support come along.

The best way to remain a master of your money is by giving it away. It helps keep a healthy perspective on whose it is, and can also have the pleasant side effect of transforming lives around the world, welcoming heaven onto earth and engaging with a God who is fundamentally generous.

The tough bit is battling with the part of you that says how much you deserve the entirety of your paycheck. You've gone through a minimum of three years hard study to get this far. You deserve this, don't you? One of Jesus' kingdom stories was about three servants (Matthew 25:14-30; Luke 19:12-28). Each was given a different amount of money by their master. The good and faithful ones used theirs wisely; one did not. If you count yourself a servant in God's kingdom, you will understand that all you have is on loan and you'll be asked to give an account of what you did with it.

The principle of tithing ten per-cent of our income is a good bench-mark, however generous generosity (not the sort measured out to the penny with a calculator) is key and it takes practice. Whether you have a lot or a little, get into the habit of giving now. It's not a pattern that grows with age if you don't start by practising it early.

"When I got my first job I really had no idea what to do with all the money I suddenly had – I wasted so much of it on rubbish."
– Adrian, 25

"Saving back some of my income for those in need enabled me to give a young mother who was about to be evicted from her home enough cash to pay her rent arrears. It was about a week's wages, but because I tithed, the money was available. What a beautiful thing to have the privilege of being part of."
– Emma, 28

Graduation - Anna

Our God is a God of celebration and parties. In Luke 15:23, he proclaims: 'Let's have a feast and celebrate!' I truly believe that at each milestone (even tiny victories in your life that nobody else would recognise), we should celebrate! We should stick a flag in the ground and say: 'I made it. Let's have a party'.

Congratulations on graduating! It is likely that your university has organised a day packed full of photos, good food and ceremony for your family and friends. Before you go, take some time to reflect on your last years at university, how far you have come, the friendships, the hard times and the good times – the years that have shaped you into who you are in this very moment now. It marks the end of one season and the beginning of another. Thank God for it. And what better way to end and begin a season than with a celebration?

Oh, and don't forget to celebrate with relatives who have faithfully supported you, as well as your mates.

Guidance - James

Growing up is about learning to stand on your own two feet and taking responsibility for yourself and the decisions you make. Spiritual maturity is no different. Some Christians seem incapable of putting one foot in front of the other without some divine and miraculous helping hand.

God has already given you the raw materials you need to make your way in this world, and 2000 years of Christian tradition and practice have set the boundaries within which you can do your own thing if seeking God's kingdom remains for you a top priority. Trust in the abilities God has given you and the dreams and desires he has put in your heart.

Of course, as a servant in the kingdom of God, your life is not your own and you should always be open to your master's particular bidding. Chances are, though, he'll just let you get on with it, happy that you are making mature choices. Only with hindsight will you see his gentle guidance throughout the course of your journey.

Healthy Eating - Anna

We live in a culture and time of plenty. Fast food restaurants await us at every corner, and tasty treats tempt us from shelves in almost every shop we walk into. We reach for them when hungry, angry, lonely, happy... food seems to satiate both our physical and emotional needs.

It's good to enjoy what we eat. The Bible tells of celebration after celebration in which people dined together. Eating was a pivotal part of culture - something to be enjoyed, something to spend time doing. And to be honest, I think we can learn a lesson from them! So, for a moment, scrap the opinions of the diet books, websites, specialists, celebrities and magazines, and let's take a look at some principles of biblical eating.

Back then, they didn't have the processed products, the additives, the packaged goods with sell-by dates that reached years into the distant future. They ate fresh fruit, vegetables and meats. They ate not only to fuel their body, but they ate in community, sharing what they had cooked - enjoying the produce that they toiled for. So, here are my biblical eating tips:

+ Eat together. Enjoy the catch-up and conversation that happens over mealtimes.

+ If it's packaged or processed, search for fresher options if you can.

+ Don't just by tins and jars - make your own pasta sauces and curry pastes.

+ If you are lucky enough to have a garden – plant some vegetables! It's both enjoyable and rewarding... not to mention healthy.

+ Think of signing up to a fresh vegetable scheme with your neighbours or housemates. It not only supports local farmers, but you'll get a surprise mix of produce each week, encouraging you to get creative in the kitchen!

+ Shop at your local market to get fresher produce that hasn't necessarily travelled half way across the world.

+ If you need speedy meals – stir-fries are perfect. Or cook bigger batches of your favourite meals and pop it into the freezer in portion sized tupperware.

+ Experiment with grains as alternatives to processed breads. My new favourites are quinoa and barley.

+ Spend time cooking and enjoying the process of creating food that you feel proud of!

+ Eat fresh! Visit the BBC's Good Food website for lots of healthy and quick recipes.

Finally, learn to listen to your body and take note of your attitudes. Make yourself accountable to others if you feel that food is a problem in your life, or if you struggle with self-control around food (both too little or too much). 1 Corinthians 6:19-20 tells us to honour our body as a temple of the Holy Spirit – eating healthily is certainly one way of doing this.

Hector - Alexander

Hi ladies. A man at work spotted you walking into the office on your first day. He knows you're out to impress your new peers. Let's call this man Hector. Though some of the girls at work are aware of his sharking ways, they don't feel they can tell you about him, because Hector is a friend of the boss. In fact, he's your line manager.

He is perfectly in his right to demand your attention anytime of the day. He can call a meeting with you and even phone you at home to go over some of the figures.

Hector is not a monster. He is quite charming at times and doesn't look that bad all in all.

As a man who works with men all over the UK, let me give you some good advice. If at any moment you feel like Hector is taking advantage of you, challenge him tactfully but firmly. Don't be afraid to stand up for yourself. And if this is something that carries on, use the HR mechanisms available to you to officially report it.

Do not let anyone take advantage of you verbally, emotionally or physically – ever. You're a daughter of the one who created all things. Your dad is the Daddy. And the Daddy is not afraid of Hector.

And guys, we are not exempt from being on the receiving end sometimes too. The same advice stands: speak up, share it, sort it.

Hidden - George

For at least the first year of your career, probably two to three, your experience of status and influence will be noticeably different from the one you'll have had at uni. At uni, people believe in the power of young adults. Campus societies are controlled and headed up by students, with budgets running into the thousands and the power to change the world of those around them. If you belonged to a society or a church without someone noticing your potential and placing you in a position of some responsibility, then you're probably in the minority.

See, in the world of education, it's all about potential. People talk about it all the time. They talk about what you could achieve in ten years' time. The problem is, you've got to work for the first few years before you can get to the tenth that people talk about.

As a final year student, you get to feel like the top of the pile. And when you start a job, you're back to the bottom of not only a new pile, but a pile where the tops are inhabited by people a lot older than you. The pile just got a lot bigger. The ladder was no longer three years from first year to graduate, but perhaps thirty years to the top of the pile. Ouch.

It can be the same in church too. You could have been part of a church used to utilising the gifts of the young people that attended.

You might have been part of a student movement or organisation, like the Christian Union, where your gifts were appreciated and opportunities to exercise them were frequent and varied.

If you move to a non-university town after you graduate, it can be a different story and it can be really difficult to adjust to churches that don't have as much experience of, or confidence in, the gifts and abilities of young adults.

In these times, it's important not to miss the benefit of being hidden. You may feel as though you're grinding away at work, with your efforts going unnoticed. The truth is that God sees everything. Seeds wait for ages under the soil and do some of their most exhausting work unseen. By the time they break through to the surface, the hardest work has been done. Be faithful in the small things, especially when no one is watching.

Hobbies - Sarah-Jane

At university you have so much time to commit to established hobbies or explore new things. Whether you were into Ultimate Frisbee, Political Debating or Medieval Re-enactment there was a society for everything and a bunch of great people to do it with.

Once you enter the working world and your amount of leisure time is dramatically reduced, it's very easy to let all of this slip. Too quickly, evening after evening can be spent lethargically flopped in front of some bad TV and life becomes about work and only work.

It's so important that you find time to do the things you love. Your eccentric interests are a part of you to be celebrated – they add colour to the fabric of life. So get up from in front of the TV and hunt out that Viking costume!

Holy - Sarah-Jane

The Bible tells us that as followers of a holy God, we should be holy in all that we do. The Message paraphrases it like this, 'As obedient children, let yourselves be pulled into a way of life shaped by God's life, a life energetic and blazing with holiness' (1 Peter 1:13-16).

Holiness in all of life. Sometimes though, it is tempting to believe that only some things really matter to God. Like overseas mission, our quiet times and giving to charity. It's much harder to see how the everyday humdrum parts of life can also be a holy offering to God.

But they really can be! There are not some bits of life that are 'sacred' and others that can remain 'secular'. Jesus is interested in our entire lifestyle – our whole being – and we can serve him wherever we are and whatever we do. Are there areas of your life that you are holding away from God at the moment? How might you seek to obey God in that area of life?

And don't just pray when you have an interview, but get into a rhythm of chatting to God throughout your working day. Don't just share testimonies from what happened when you helped on the Alpha Course, but what God was teaching you on your course at work. See him in everything.

Blaze with holiness.

"You are placed in your work for a reason and you are to be Jesus in that place. Never slip into thinking that your time at work is less significant than your voluntary work for the church." – Amy, 26

Honesty - James

This is a hard one. Whether it's a slight fudging of the truth or the most blatant of lies, you are being naïve if you think you're not going to come across (or be asked to take part in) some dodgy dealings from time to time. From misleading hype about the products you're selling, to spinning a web of half-truths about financial information – or simply taking a day-off you're not entitled to – dishonesty, to some degree or another, is rife. When you start work, you're going to have to make a judgment call on what you're going to do when you're faced with it. Sometimes it will even feel like you will lose out by telling the truth.

There's no fudging the issue according to the Bible. 'Truth' is synonymous with good; 'lies' are synonymous with evil. The choice to be honest or deceitful is a choice between God and the devil (who John describes as the 'father of lies', John 8:44). We either walk in the light or we walk in darkness.

So, be honest at all times, in all your dealings. Remember though, you can only make that choice for yourself; you can't always make it on behalf of your colleagues. It's clear-cut, in theory. It's applying the theory that's the tricky bit. How will you persuade your work colleagues that honesty is the best policy? Lead by example and rest in the knowledge that God's first call in your life is for YOU to love him with everything.

"In my very first job I was asked to write a fake CV which said that I had two years more experience than I actually did so that my company might win a consultancy contract. I felt really uncomfortable doing this, so returned the work with this part left out. It was a bit awkward with my manager at first, but after a while I got a name for myself as someone who wasn't prepared to lie and never got asked to again." – Jeremy, 25

"In my first job there was great pressure to lie to customers in order to avoid extra work for me and my colleagues and to mis-sell products. It wasn't easy resisting such temptation." – George, 24

House Sharing - Liz

If living on your own seems financially unviable or even just unthinkable then consider house sharing. It may not be a good idea to rent with other students unless you are continuing education yourself. People in work tend to keep very different hours to those studying and the two can be difficult to reconcile. Do you really want to be woken up at 2.30am in the morning mid-week when they have all just got back from a night out? Do they really want to be woken up at 7am when you are pottering around getting ready for work?

Human - Sarah-Jane

"We're all human."

Sounds obvious right? But it's not always how we treat people. Sometimes when there is a job to be done (at work, at home or even, yes, at church) we can be so focused on the task that we don't see the beautiful, God-imaged individuals before our very eyes. So, ask God to help you to remember the human.

Remembering the human looks like stopping to help a mother down the tube steps with the buggy in rush hour, even if it will make you a few minutes late. It looks like noticing a colleague seems stressed at work and going to see if you can help lighten the load. It looks like not getting angry when someone doesn't turn up for their rota slot at church, but instead wondering if they are OK and shooting up a prayer.

The world may sometimes tell you that you are just a number, a cog in the machine of life, but you are a unique and precious individual. Have eyes for the unique and precious individuals around you.

As Oxfam say, let's be human-kind.

"It can be hard to put relationships before getting the job done when the pressure is on. I have to stop and remind myself to think about the person before the task."
- Gemma, 25

"Love the one in front of you. Even when all around is changing, in terms of one's daily activities and relationships, you are still surrounded by God's children. As you meet each one in the Father, the Father meets you through each one." - Rupert, 27

Identity - George

Working can throw up real issues and challenges about your identity, and this is in no small way down to the system of labelling that our society practises. Now there are, broadly, two types of label: the 'Dinner Party Label' and the 'Salary Slip Label'.

The 'Dinner Party Label' is the answer that you give when somebody at a dinner party asks what you do for a living. At the moment, I get to say that I'm an advertising scriptwriter, and so people usually go, 'Ooooh, I bet that's exciting... Do you know the Meerkat?' etc. The acid test with the 'Dinner Party Label' is how you feel about the title you give yourself when it comes out of your mouth. Do you wince as you say 'hedge fund manager' or 'compensation solicitor'? Do you barely bring your eyes from your drink as your explain that you work in the post room, or as a bin man? Do you relish the look on people's faces when you tell them you're a celebrity psychoanalyst, or a cancer-cure research scientist? If your response is any of the above, then you've already bought into the modern lie that these labels actually carry any weight. Your identity is not tied solely to what you do.

Your primary definition comes from the One who made you and the One in whom you are hidden. Nothing else. People can beat or build themselves up about labels that ultimately aren't the deciding factor about who they are.

The 'Salary Slip Label' is the label you give yourself when you open your wage slip at the end of the month, and again, the way you feel about it. If it begins to affect your understanding of your identity so that you begin to say either: "I'm worth more than this, my work is worth more, I can't believe he or she is worth more," or "Yeah, that's about right, I've worked hard for this, I deserve it, I'm glad they've recognised me, I'm definitely worth this much," then you've also bought into a lie.

Letting either of these two labels stick to you can be destructive and can become a place where the enemy will love to heap lie upon lie into your head. Remember where you come from, practise the spiritual disciplines like Sabbath, fasting, or the discipline taught to the Jews in Deuteronomy 26:5, where they recited their history whenever they reaped. These two lies are some of the most pervasive in modern times, and the sooner you kick them into touch, the better.

One of the best ways to do combat the belief that your job shapes your identity, or what you do is who you are, is to take your Sabbath well. The Sabbath is a time when you stop working and find that you're OK just as you are, removed from the context of labour and put into your place where God alone defines you. You remind yourself that you are a human being, not a human doing.

"Even though I am confident that the job I'm in is where God has called me to be, I can still slip into comparing myself to my peers with ridiculous questions like 'How are they progressing?', 'Are they being paid more than me?', 'Have they been given management responsibility earlier than me?'" – Jay, 30

Independence - Liz

You've been independent for such a long time now and in graduating it's time to take another leap into independence. This may feel like a frightening thought or you may feel totally liberated! You may decide on further study or the world of work, you may even be setting up your own business. Whatever it is you are planning, you're now carving out the next phase of your journey.

Independence means choices – choices to decide who you are going to be and how you are going to live, with less pressure to do what other people think you ought to. Relish that freedom and don't let your thinking be confined to the few options that have been presented to you as 'expected' in the past.

But at the same time, being a Christian means that absolute independence is never really the goal. We love a God that asks us to live in relationship with him every step of the way and to live in community. We are called to be radically interdependent – to share stuff, time, life with one another because we know that ultimately it is not our own.

So be brave. Seek God. And talk through your ideas with people who love and know you, people whose opinions you really trust.

"Seek community. Have a group of unwavering Christian friends. Journey together into the world of work." - Aaron, 23

"Don't forget to look after others – becoming self-centred because you are always focussed on yourself is the worst way to end up once starting work." - Katie, 24

Interviews - Sarah-Jane

Ah, interviews! How is it possible to hope for something so much and also dread it so much at the same time?!

You may not have had very many interviews up until this point, so it will take a little while for you to get your head around what interviewers are actually after. Preparation is key. You can't expect to be able to answer all of the questions well on the day spontaneously without having put in some decent forethought.

All interviewers will have some specific questions of their own, but most will likely cover the following:

+ Why do you want the job? What appeals about the role and the company?

+ How do your skills (specifically) match those required in the job description? Identify the key competencies required (e.g. time management, problem solving, leadership) and memorise an example for each.

+ How will you be able to use your past experience in the new role?

+ What kind of worker are you? Do you enjoy working in a team or prefer to get on with your work independently?

+ What are your top two strengths and weaknesses? (Can you twist the weakness into something positive by showing a lesson you have learnt?)

+ How would you react on the job if things went wrong?

+ What are your ambitions? Where do you see yourself in five years' time?

For each question, try to illustrate the point you make with a real-life example. For instance, rather than just saying, "I enjoy working in a team and think I am a natural leader", why not prove your point by recalling a story from your gap year when you led your team through a tricky situation? When preparing for interview, try to create a pool of examples that you can fall back on if you suddenly dry up.

At the end of the interview you will almost always be asked if you have any questions to ask of your interviewers. Again, preparation is key. Write a list of thoughtful questions ahead of time. You may have practical questions about when you would need to start, or what your salary would be, or you may have broader questions about the company's ethos or approach to staff development. Don't ever ask anything that you could have found out on their website though – that just shows that you haven't done your homework thoroughly enough!

I needn't have to say that dressing smartly is essential. Shirts need to be ironed, shoes polished, nails clipped, hair styled and breath freshened! Looking good should boost your confidence too.

It's inevitable that you're going to feel a bit nervous, but as Christians we shouldn't have to be crippled by worry. If we commit our interviews to God in prayer (and actually let go and put it in his hands, rather than just praying "Lord, please let me get the job") we can rest in the knowledge that he will make our paths straight whether we get the job or not (Proverbs 3:6). In the current job market it is likely that you will have to suffer a fair number of rejections before signing your first contract. Try not to take each one too personally and don't torture yourself by going through all of the answers that you could have given.

Prepare well. Offer it to God. Do your best. Trust.

"Employers look for people who have constructive, positive attitudes – who 'see the glass as half full'. Your attitude can really set you apart at interview in a good way."
– Esther, 29

"Think long-term. When in interviews, ask yourself, 'Are these nice people? Would spending time with them be mutually beneficial?" – Isabel, 30

Insomnia - Alexander

To quote the band Faithless: 'There's no release, I'm wide awake in my kitchen, it's dark and I'm lonely, oh if I could only get some sleep, creaky noises make my skin creep, I need to get some sleep, I can't get no sleep.'

Though insomnia provides great inspiration for Al Pacino films and epic 1990s songs, it also affects real-life humans. Causes of insomnia vary from fickle changes of habits to deep-rooted issues. But the fact remains that if you do not find a regular sleeping pattern your working pattern will suffer. One or two sleepless nights doesn't warrant a trip to the doctor, but if it becomes more of a regular unwanted issue, get yourself to the GP.

God designed rest to be good for us. It's so vital, even God does it.

"My one piece of advice for the working world: Go to sleep earlier!" – David, 30

Integrity - George

Integrity is a massive challenge. It is what people will notice first and let you forget last. It will be the thing that stings when you abandon it. You will meet daily challenges to it and the worldviews of those around you will assault it.

What I find most inspiring is a line from the vision from the 24/7 Prayer movement. It says of our generation:

'They gave up the game of minimum integrity long ago to reach for the stars.'

It can be so easy to settle for 'minimum integrity', to just scrape by. Don't. Be excellent. Get in shape now, because life will only get harder and busier. Be faithful in the small things.

"Work as hard and as well as you can. Offer your employer quality for your wages and you will find favour from both your boss and God. Your witness will be blessed as people see how you work with integrity." – James, 22

Intentionality - George

Exercise prayerful intentionality. It's probably the key to lessening the negative effects of having less free time and energy. Your time is a precious resource when you start working and the possibility of achieving things without much arrangement, due to the spontaneous nature that free time affords, doesn't really work when you have a 9 to 5 job. If you think things that you want are going to 'just happen', then they probably won't. If you get home, and haven't got any plans then the likelihood is that you'll have tea, feel pretty wiped, watch a bit of telly, and before you know it, it's half 9, and you've got to go to bed in an hour.

Basically, if you want something to happen, whether it's a project you want to achieve or a new friendship or prayer, put things in place to make it happen, or it probably won't. If you want it, plan it in, set targets, do things purposefully. The reason I call it prayerful intentionality is that those things which you set about doing should also be the things that God wants you to do. After you're sure that's what he wants you to do, go for it.

"Don't try and do everything that you were doing as a student – there just isn't time! Prioritise or burn out." – Nikki, 21

Isolation - Liz

Post-university life can be a difficult time for some people in which they feel isolated, especially if you are unprepared as I was. At university it felt like everyone was right alongside me, as we all had the same things in common – exams, essay deadlines etc. At work other people's issues felt daunting and their busy lives seemed to have little room for me. Try to prepare yourself that your daily life will look a lot different after graduation. Take the initiative in keeping in touch with friends and let people know when you are feeling out on a limb.

"I found it really hard to develop genuine fellowship when entering a new church. You don't realise how precious the deep relationships cultivated at university are until they are taken away from you." – Dean, 26

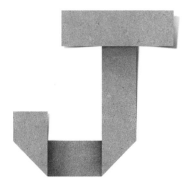

Jobs - Sarah-Jane

If you are in your final year, there's probably little taking more of your head space right now than your exams and what job you are going to do next year. And once you start working, your job will not only take up such a huge part of your head space, but also your time. This means that the workplace is now your primary place to serve God. Think of it as your service of God, your worship to God and your mission field for God all at once. Let me explain:

Work has instrumental value – through our work we get things done that make God smile. People are fed, children are taught, and products are made...things that add to the flourishing of mankind. God values your work, because the thing you do is itself valuable.

Work has intrinsic value – through our work we express our praise and worship to God by using the gifts and talents that he has given us. God values your work, because it can be an act of worship.

Work has strategic value – our workplaces are a context for God's mission. At work we can minister to others, we can influence office culture and be a witness to our colleagues. God values your work because he can use you there.

So whether you are going into your dream job, or are having to take something not ideal for the time being, remember that you are working for God. 'Whatever you do, work at it with all your heart, as working for the Lord.' (Colossians 3:23)

"I found out the hard way that you can't blag your way through work! The stuff you got away with at uni – procrastination, poor time management, lateness – will get you nowhere at work! Raise your game – there are no resists in the working world!" – Joe, 24

"Work is really valuable – it will stretch you in new ways, challenge you and help you develop. It's a great adventure!" – Esther, 27

Kit Kat - Alexander

Wherever you work, there will be those who snack from dawn until dusk. Keep an eye out for the cakes and chocolates which will surface around you daily. A moment on the lips, a lifetime on the hips = countless gym trips.

"No-one warned me before I started work of the sheer gluttony in offices! You would not believe the amount of chocolates, biscuits and sweets there are!" – K, 28

Lounge - Alexander

Wherever you live after you leave university, make sure you dedicate some significant time to keeping at least one room in your house impeccably tidy. The last thing you want is to return home from a hard day at that office to be welcomed by cereal bowls filled with mouldy matter, empty bottles of wine and torn envelopes strewn across the living room floor.

A clean lounge makes it easier to offer spontaneous hospitality and one of the best feelings on a Friday evening is falling into your sofa knowing full well that the weekend has arrived with no major cleaning to do.

Also, on a Sunday night take a few minutes to plan the big events of the week ahead. This way you'll feel on top of the big stuff before Monday morning comes knocking.

Love - James

No, we're not tiptoeing through the minefield of office romances here (we'd need a whole book for that); we're thinking about the compassionate love we should have for everyone we meet, including our enemies (and you might make a few at work).

Perverse though they sometimes sound, and hard though they often are to live out, God's principles do actually work. It might take a long time before you see any opportunities, but if you can love your enemies and bless those who denigrate you, you will be amazed at the results. Compassionate, no-strings-attached love is powerfully counter-cultural.

Marriage - Sarah-Jane

For a fair few couples that have been dating throughout their time at university, graduating can mean thinking seriously about marriage. Getting married young, as I did, can be a wonderful thing – an adventure in which you go through the big life changes hand in hand as a new family unit. It also means that making big decisions about jobs and where to live are all a bit more complicated! Everything now involves two people – you can no longer just think of yourself.

If you have been talking about marriage but have some nagging hesitations, take some time to talk and pray them through with your partner and maybe a trusted third party. Getting married is not something to enter into lightly. Remember, there's no rush and it is far better to voice concerns now rather than two years into being Mr and Mrs!

If you're engaged, get a couple you respect to lead you through some marriage preparation or find your nearest Marriage Course. Having a structure to talk through the deep things of life really helps to make sure you are both on the same page with your expectations for what married life will be like. However head-over-heels you feel right now, you'll also really benefit from the important communication tools for the challenges that marriage will inevitably throw your way.

And if marriage is still a long way off for you right now, support your friends who are tying the knot. For many newlyweds adjusting to a new way of life can be hard, especially for the first year of marriage. It may feel like they are the ones who get all the perks (bed buddies, gift lists and honeymoons!), but the reality is that wider society benefits when a couple has a strong marriage.

Mexican - Alexander

Treat yourself from time-to-time. Hunt down the best restaurant in your town and try to have a cheeky meal there a few times a month. Get to know the staff. Try the whole menu. Variety is the spice of life and Mexican food has become one of my most recent discoveries. Make sure it's local to where you live and maybe try to find one which doesn't belong to a chain. There's something beautiful about supporting small businesses striving for excellence. You might find you're on a permanent discount if you attend regularly enough, which allows you to tip the staff even more!

Neglect - Alexander

Let me offend you. When you finally close/burn/shelve your books and the idea of studying anything else is about as appealing as a major operation...why not start studying again? The irony of leaving full-time studies is that you finally have enough time to read things that you choose yourself. I love that I can study new things in my own time now that I have my evenings free.

Once you get your first set of letters after your name, see it as your opportunity to learn something new. Why not have a look at your local college website to see what part-time evening courses are on offer? You have time to learn another language now, or how make your own pasta sauce. Whatever you do, try not to neglect the brain God has given you. What new skill would you like to learn?

Neighbours - Anna

At university we were used to people living a more 24-hour lifestyle. You would let it slide a little if your neighbours were up partying into the early hours or if your housemate stumbled in and woke you whilst cooking a must-have cheese toasty.

In Luke 10:27 we are told to love our neighbours – let's take this literally. How can we really love those who live around us? We live so close to one another, yet names can be unknown and conversations can be little more than an obligatory nod.

Get to know names and faces. Invite people round! If you love baking, bake impromptu gifts.

Organise a road party, throw a mince pies and mulled wine evening. Get creative.

Once, I came home to a note on the entrance of our block of flats saying, 'Can the person who put their washing machine on at 11pm please refrain from doing so'. Now this individual must have known it was me. They lived below me! It would have been their ceiling that shook whilst our washing machine slowly made its way across the floor on spin cycle. But instead of slipping a discrete note under our door, they decided to make it clear to the whole block!

Despite being irritated at her public way of going about it, I decided to react in the opposite spirit. So, I wrote back and pinned it up for all to see. 'Hi, so sorry for the noise last night. Love number 10'.

Surprise people with friendliness, intrigue people with kindness and seek friendship without agenda. What could you do for your neighbours?

Newbie - Sarah-Jane

Whether we like it or not, first impressions count. They say that the conversation you have with someone in the first five minutes will shape a person's impression of you for the whole of your future relationship.

So how are you going to introduce yourself on your first day? Will your body language give the impression that you are enthusiastic and excited to be there or that you wish you could still be in bed?

And which bits of information about yourself will you choose to disclose? Maybe a bit about what you studied at uni, your family or where you grew up? What about that Christian gap year you had? Or that you went to church on Sunday or don't live with your long-term girl/boyfriend? Listen to God's prompting. There are tons of natural ways to let people know that you are a Christian and the sooner you do it, the easier it will be.

Oh, and if you have a disastrous first five minutes – arrive covered in bird poo and have the most awkward conversation ever – do not fear. All is not lost! Our God is a God of second chances, so have a laugh about it, take a deep breath and try again on day two.

"Start as you mean to go on. Be yourself and there should be heaps of natural opportunities to let people know you follow Jesus." – Chris, 29

Office Politics - George

There's only so long that you can keep up an attitude of innocence and naivety, because sooner or later the issues will involve and affect you. The question is: How can you have integrity in these situations?

Firstly, lots of office politics involves gossip. The way to work with this is to ask for Jesus' eyes for these people. The way gossip functions is to say that 'people don't change'. That person always does that kind of thing, and they'll only carry on doing it and getting worse. The gospel says that's categorically not true. It says that people can be redeemed, can be changed into the likeness of Christ. The good news is that whatever is said about a person isn't the last word on them.

Secondly, know that it's OK to speak up when you see injustice. The real test of your integrity is being able to say the same things when called into the boss' office, when it can really make a difference, and not just when letting off steam with colleagues in the kitchen. If something is not right, don't just moan about it in the gossip sessions but pray through how you could take action to see something change.

"If you are going to take a stand on an issue, do it in a way that maintains relationship – there's no point in trying to lead if nobody follows." – Pete, 25

Oliver - Alexander

Buck the trend in your new job. Be content. If you are on a graduate scheme or a traineeship of some kind, everyone will know how much you're getting paid. Don't worry about it. Your boss will remind you that a pay rise will be coming in a bid to keep you at the company and provide incentive for nailing your targets.

Whenever you get a bonus or a Christmas secret santa, be content. Enjoy what you have been given. It won't take long until your once glamorous pay packet feels like a single bowl of gruel to Oliver Twist. Being content in God with what you have in the moment is one of the major keys to wisdom (Philippians 4:5-12).

That said, if you are being exploited, take the initiative to negotiate a reasonable pay-rise. It's entirely appropriate to expect to be paid in line with the going rates for your sector. Don't be greedy, but don't be a doormat.

Ouch! - James

Not everyone you'll work with will share your values. Maybe no-one will. Some 'colleagues' won't think twice about stitching you up to get ahead. Office politics can be a tricky path to negotiate. It can get nasty; it can get personal. One thing is for sure: you'll find out how deep your values really go.

So, do you give up now and resign yourself to a flat-lining career trajectory or do you give as good you get? Well, that's something you're going to have to work out for yourself. However, when Jesus first sent out his disciples to announce that 'The kingdom of heaven is near' (Matthew 10:7), he knew he was sending them out 'like sheep among wolves'. He gave them this piece of advice: 'Be as shrewd as snakes and as innocent as doves.' In today's language it would go something like this: 'Wise up, but don't stoop to their level.' Remember, we play by a different set of rules and we judge winning or losing by a different set of values.

P.S. Don't think that because you've applied to work for a Christian organisation that you'll be immune. People are people – and self-interest is self-interest – wherever you are and however it is dressed up.

"Stand alongside your colleagues – don't step on anyone to get ahead!" – Chris, 29

Pace - Liz

Whatever avenue you decide to take next, whether pursuing work or further study, the pace of life will undoubtedly change. You may start to keep very different hours and be away from home much longer, especially if you have a long commute. Adjusting to a new pace of life can be challenging. Don't worry if you find the change of gear tiring at first – you will adjust in time. Try to seek out those who are doing similar things to you. Share experiences and don't isolate yourself.

"Don't panic if you mourn the loss of your social life and all that free time to pack with reading, friends and serving. In work you have to be more conscious about what you do with your time, but that's OK too. You are not failing at multi-tasking, you are just moving on." – Anna, 25

"Don't expect yourself to master juggling this new lifestyle without practice. You'll get better at it in time." – Owen, 26

Parents:
Living Away From Them - George

Living away from parents is kind of what you were built to do. But interestingly, it's kind of not what they were built to do. They're wired to worry, which helps when you're two, but not so much when you're twenty-two. Truth is, they can't help it.

They'll want to call and check and fuss. That's OK – love them with your attention, and understand that they're calling for their own sake as much as they are for yours. A few decades down the line you'll probably be the one calling your own child to ask if they have enough sleep/money/greens.

Remember, just because you are an independent adult now, it doesn't mean you stop being a son or daughter. Why not try being the one that calls them once in a while?

Parents:
Living With Them - Liz

You've not been living with them for quite some time and now you may have to make the decision whether or not to go back home. But – stop. Think before you do. You're not the same person that left three or four years ago, and neither are your parents. Consider how you've changed and how that might affect the dynamics. It would also be wise to consider what living with your parents might be like now – what boundaries might you need to put in place in order to maintain a healthy relationship?

Going back to your parents can be done successfully if that's where you need to go. Over the past fifteen years since graduating, I've been back three times to lodge with my parents, twice with my husband. If the expectations are set out beforehand – the length, the rent, the chores – then living with your parents again can bring a welcome respite wherever you are on your journey.

"I felt like I had gone back a step when I moved back in with my parents. It was so easy to act like a teenager again and they treated me that way too. This is where grace and patience are tested. Be ready to communicate when you feel patronised and always be grateful for your parents."
- Joe, 27

Promotion - Alexander

For lots of graduates, the first two years of full-time employment are quite frankly a slog with few perks. However, some of you will soon be faced with the notion of promotion. It may sound like an alien term to you at just 21, but as companies downsize and bosses look more and more to new ideas and fresh passion to drive the firm forward, you will be considered if you have the right attitude.

So, office politics aside, you will have to weigh up big decisions in a relatively short amount of time after leaving university comforts. The biggest challenge for a Christian in the workplace is the thin line between working as hard as you can as if Christ was your boss and idolising a shiny career path until you become the boss. For any of us looking to start a family, we all have to take on board a counter-cultural approach to priorities.

Many men and women are paying the price for relegating their families to the bottom of the priority list. Don't get me wrong, work is very important. God has created us to work. The first man and woman worked in Eden. However, we need to stay alert that we do not worship the created by taking our eyes off the creator.

Is taking a promotion wrong? Absolutely not. Is sacrificing all other priorities for your life to get a promotion? Absolutely.

"Don't put money, security, promotion, buying a house, settling down, starting a family as your priorities so that they become a ladder of aims that distract you from growing as God's servant." – Roland, 28

Puff - Alexander

Though you have proven you can study one subject to a great depth and construct good arguments and sound opinions, don't become too proud of your academic achievements. 'Knowledge puffs up,' Paul the Apostle warns. In fact, when someone enquires about your degree, speak humbly about your achievements. Consider those around you before yourself. Find out about the achievements of others and enquire about them. Learn about John's interest in ancient history, Sarah's third year speaking Spanish in Murcia and Ray's prized allotment at the back of his council house.

The temptation is to fly out of university with your degree stapled to your head, reminding people you have cleaned the floor with your lecturers. Be slow to speak about what you have done but quick to talk about where you want to go. Vision is often crippled by nostalgia. The need to revisit past milestones usually highlights present insecurities.

Purpose - Sarah-Jane

Some days, when work is tiresome and it seems like you are going two steps backwards for every one you take forwards, it's easy to see where the writer of Ecclesiastes was coming from when he moans, 'What do workers gain from their toil? Everything is meaningless'. In other words, 'What is the point?'

It's a very good question and one that left unanswered can lead to both a lack of motivation and a lack of fulfilment. So why do you do the job that you do? Or why are you applying to do the kind of work that you are? To earn a living – yes. To do something you enjoy – hopefully, yes. But does your work carry any higher purpose too?

Every workplace will have its own culture and will champion different 'purposes' – a business might champion profit, whilst a government department might champion 'progress'. The challenge is to learn to see through these to the kingdom purposes behind, to how God might be using your field to work out his own purposes. Is your business creating wealth for many and providing good products and services to customers that help them flourish? Is your government department working on policies that bring about justice and work for the common good?

The writer of Ecclesiastes goes on to conclude that, if looked at in purely earthly terms, work is, at the end of the day, pretty meaningless, but if seen as part of the eternal kingdom that God is building then finding satisfaction through work is actually a gift from God (Ecclesiastes 3:12-14). Whether medicine or banking or teaching or sales, how is the work that you do being used by God in the building of his lasting kingdom? It's a big question, well worth wrestling.

"I missed the excitement of meeting with Christian friends almost every day and having a constant sense of being on mission that was formed though the close fellowship at university – back then it was easier to feel like I was part of something bigger."
– James, 27

"It can be really hard to stay positive in a pressurised and demanding work environment. Try to keep in mind a clear idea of how your line of work renews the world and brings the kingdom – you are part of something bigger."
– Andy, 26

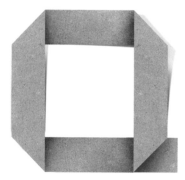

Quiz - Alexander

If you didn't do this at university, do it now! Get a group of three friends together and make the ultimate pub quiz team. It's a great way to share your faith with those around you whilst laughing out your DNA at some of the questions you get wrong. The local pub is one of the best parts of British culture. Remember the names of the bar staff and those who prop up the bar. Many Christians still believe that one of the Ten Commandments reads: Thou shall not enter into a building serving wine, beer or KP Nuts! Instead, join in with the wholesome bits of the banter and use it to show the locals that following Jesus actually includes living life to the full.

Redundancy - Anna

The recession threw people into panic! People who had never questioned the safety of their jobs had the rugs pulled from under their feet. It can happen.

I was made redundant from my first job in advertising. The reality of it was that I didn't know how I was going to pay rent. But one thing I did sense was an underlying peace that came from a knowledge that God doesn't get taken by surprise.

If you ever find yourself having been made redundant, there are three things I would suggest:

+ Lean into God. He says "Do not fear" in the Bible 366 times. That's one for each day of the year, even in a leap year! Pray with others for an increase in faith and trust.

+ Make use of the resources and help available to you from the state. I was fortunately only out of work for a month, but I had the very humbling experience of going on the dole. I would sit in a room full of suited parents who had no idea as to how they were going to keep up mortgage and schooling payments.

+ Turn your lack of work into a full-time job. My job was - to get a job. I fixed up my CV, met with agencies, hounded people for interviews and would sit in coffee shops in my interview outfit ready for impromptu slots!

God might not be responsible for our circumstances, but he is faithful, and has an amazing way of turning messy situations into powerful testimonies. Your God is the God that parted the Red Sea, the God that heals, the God that even death can't touch. And he is here, he is capable... and he doesn't get taken by surprise.

Responsible - James

What a grown-up word. While we don't want you getting old before your time, the sooner you start taking on some responsibility the quicker you'll start moving into the exciting things life's got to offer. Don't just simply mark time; that's such a waste of a good life.

It's a state of mind, as much as anything. Make that choice and you'll be amazed at what you see happen. You might be the only Christian where you end up working; in which case, step up to the plate. Decide to take spiritual responsibility for the group you work with. Pastor them — be a friend to them; pray for them; be ready with a word for them, should the opportunity arise. Go to work every day in the knowledge that you have the transforming word of life inside of you.

Rest - Sarah-Jane

We were designed to rest. We are made in the image of a God who rested after six days of creation and who gave us the Sabbath as a life-refreshing gift. It's a gift that says, 'It's OK to slow down, I've got you.' During the biblical years when work was mostly agricultural, to take a day off was costly. By obeying the instruction to keep the Sabbath even during the ploughing season and harvest (Exodus 34:21), the Israelites demonstrated that even if they missed a day out in the fields during the key harvest times, they were reliant on a God that would provide for their needs. For productive, driven people, rest can feel inefficient and like a waste of time. But at the heart of the practice of Sabbath is a call to humility - to stop, lay things down and reflect with the one who is really in control about what he is doing in and through us.

You'll know your body's warning signs that signal that you've pushed yourself too far. For me, my eyes go twitchy and I become (even more!) clumsy, dropping things left, right and centre, twitching as I go. If you're having to take off more than one or two sick days a year, this is probably another signal that you are not getting enough rest. How might you space out your annual leave well? When are the most stressful times in your working calendar (maybe around budget time, or during an inspection) and how might you prepare yourself ahead of time with good rest so as to avoid the normal burn out?

It's important to work out how best you rest, as we all have our own rhythms. Perhaps if you regularly have to work on Sundays you could think about taking a different day, or allocating a special evening to intentionally take time with God instead?

And remember, not everything that looks like rest is actually restful. I absolutely love spending my evenings hosting dinner parties – giving rest to others – but funnily there only a few combinations of people with whom I find this experience truly restful myself. Find what will refresh you and lead you deeper with God and be thankful for the gift of rest.

"You might never have felt the need for a structured Sabbath at uni as the student lifestyle afforded so much choice about how to spend your time. But in order to be able to sustain commitment to work, relationships, domestic jobs and church you need space and time that is set aside deliberately for rest." – Laura, 30

"Even if you work in an office with a culture of very long working hours, this doesn't have to be your culture. By working really hard and by the grace of God I've managed to gain a reputation as an efficient worker. This has enabled me to set strong boundaries on the hours I will work." – Esther, 29

Ross Kemp - Alexander

Don't become addicted to television, but don't throw it out either. Enjoy watching your favourite programmes, films or documentaries – celebrate your personal taste. But also, try to think a little more strategically about what you watch. Let me explain. On Monday mornings in every workplace across the country, staff will be chatting about at least two things: weekend antics and television. If you've been living in a Christian bubble all weekend, you'll actually find it quite difficult to join in with these chats.

So find out the key programme your colleagues are watching and consider it a missional opportunity to tune in too. People in different places of work will have different favourite shows – maybe near you it's Ross Kemp or EastEnders or the football? Have a laugh, listen to others, share your opinion and be prepared to explain why you think the way you do because of your faith in Jesus.

Also, have an informed opinion on political events. Watch the news, read the BBC website, buy a weekly newspaper or tune into Question Time. Decisions made by those in power still affect you just as much (perhaps even more) despite your exit from studentdom. The more informed you are on the events in contemporary culture, the better conversations you'll have with your workmates.

Sex - Alexander

Though you might have left one world void of sexual restraint, the working world is often not that different. Many offices are the places where some of the worst decisions are made. A vast number of marriages are torn apart by decisions made by men and women whilst at their place of work.

As Christians we are called to live above and beyond reproach when it comes to sexual morality. However, let's not be too naive to think we are immune to the temptations around us. One of the problems with sin is that it often becomes 'acceptable' in the professional world. It's almost as if some careers allow people to get away with a lot more due to the stress involved in the job.

Strangely, the only issue that the New Testament overtly commands us to 'flee from' is sexual immorality (1 Corinthians 6:18). Work socials, long lunch-breaks and half-empty offices provide ample space to find security from that member of staff who reminds you of the romance of your youth. Talk openly about your views on sex before marriage and how you value it as a beautiful gift from God, but always be ready to flee if the scope for sexual temptation increases.

Also, be ready to help improve somebody's marriage. Lots of people are fascinated by a Christian's perception of marriage. When people encounter radical believers who actually think that God delights in the institution of marriage – a committed, faithful life-long union – they encounter hope. Our purpose as followers of Jesus is often to remind people that there is hope for them in their situation.

Shifts - Sarah-Jane

Split shifts, late shifts, night shifts... the reality is that not everyone is going to be working a steady 9 to 5 job. In fact, for all of the essential services we rely on (nurses, highway maintenance workers, the police etc.) there will be someone working at any given moment.

If you're starting a job that requires you to work in irregular shift patterns, it's going to take some adjusting to. Maintaining relationships, getting enough food and sleep and relating to God all take a different kind of effort. It's easy to feel left out if you're having to work whilst everyone else is out socialising. If you are feeling this way, be open with your friends and family and pray together about how you can help your relationships to continue to flourish in this new rhythm.

Equally, if you have friends who are doing shift work – think about how you can best support them. Might you be able to meet up on your lunch break when they have a day off if evenings are difficult? Might they appreciate a text during a long shift to know that you are thinking of them? How might our church communities be more flexible to meet the needs of those who can't make a regular home group?

We rely on shift workers so much more than we know. Let's honour them by being more intentionally flexible.

"Undertaking shift work confounded my opportunities to attend the same church, the same service, or the same home group, on a regular basis, and precluded me from engaging fully in other opportunities to serve, in worship, or youth work etc."
– Rupert, 27

"A regular 'quiet time' can't happen due to my unpredictable hours, so I try to use my drive to the hospital and between visiting mums as opportunities to pray for myself and those I meet." – Ali, 28

Singleness - Sarah-Jane

If you are leaving university single and going to a flurry of friends' weddings, it can be easy to think that you have missed your one chance to find somebody. This is rubbish! The average age for marriage in the UK is 30. You are still so, so young and will meet hundreds of new people over this next decade.

Rather than letting your singleness define you, find your identity as a son or daughter of the King of all creation. Take time to discover the depth of God's love for you and build on your relationship with him so that when you do meet that special someone you'll have an inner strength and know your own self-worth.

Long-term singleness is difficult, but can have certain advantages too. Relish the freedom you have in choosing where to live and work while you are not accountable to a partner. As you move into a new job and a perhaps new church, there will be many opportunities for meeting new people. Family life, if and when it comes, will bring many restrictions and its own struggles. Enjoy this time of fewer responsibilities as you continue to grow into the person God has made you to be.

Small Fish, Big Pond - Anna

So you have gone from a cosy and familiar group of friends to a whole new environment where everyone else seems to know each other. They share in-jokes and just seeming to 'know' whose coffee mugs should be avoided and where the best places are to grab lunch.

If you feel like you are a little lost – find a friendly face and ask. Don't forget that everyone was new too at some point. I worked as a temp for two whole weeks until I found out that they had a strong penchant for filling the kettle with the special filtered water from the cooler! So it's good to ask someone for the lowdown on any office quirks!

Be patient with yourself. Be a 'yes' man (or woman, of course). Say yes to social invites and opportunities to meet new people. Why not join a team at church – one sure-fire way to get stuck in and make friends.

Stuck - Sarah-Jane

We all get stuck at some point or other in life. Stuck in bad relationships, bad jobs, bad habits – and the longer we are stuck, the harder it feels like we might ever be able to change. You'll probably know when you're stuck because there will be a constant niggling feeling that things ought to be different.

Now I'm not talking about a flighty, commitment-fearing, sense of entitlement that jumps ship as soon as things get hard. No, loyalty and the grit to stick things out are honourable qualities. Rather, I am talking about the crippling incapacity to see the possibility of change, usually brought about by a combination of bad choices, low self-esteem and fear.

If you are in a relationship that you know deep-down is not right and not going to last – don't waste another few months (or even years!). If you wake up each morning dreading going to work, stop – take some time out with trusted friends to seek where God might be able to use you better elsewhere. You might even have to take a bit of a financial hit to re-train, but it will be worth it in the end.

Don't get stuck, else you'll blink and you'll be thirty.

"Find a job that fits your personality and skills – don't stay too long in your first job if it sucks. I struggled in my first job for 3 and a half years before having the courage to seek a change. I've been in my second job for a year now and I can't believe how good work can be!" – Hugh, 28

Student Loans - Liz

Eeek, the time is approaching when you have to start paying back your student loan. This may seem like a huge debt hanging over your head but put it in perspective – when my husband and I found our feet, found jobs and were feeling a bit more like we knew where money was coming from we drew a graph of time against debt decreasing. It was a pleasant surprise to see that graph line go down every month and to know that there was an end in sight. It helped us keep on paying the debt off, to aim towards being debt free.

Success - James

Don't be afraid of it. Be the best you can at everything you do, including your work. The world of work does not exist in a vacuum. Working well is as much a spiritual endeavour as praying. Listen to the voice within. Trust your dreams. Embrace your ambition. You are the future; make yours count. Do something extraordinary. May your life be a light, especially at work – after all, over the coming decades, you're going to be spending a large chunk of time hard at it.

And if you're thinking: 'What have I got to offer?' think about this; whether it's a baby born in a stable or a small boy with five loaves and two fish given over to God, small things can produce extraordinary results.

Remember, in God's kingdom 'success' is judged by a different set of values. Like John the Baptist, be wary of taking all the kudos for yourself, and be ready to pay a temporal price for heavenly rewards. No one said the way of the cross would be easy, but it leads to true success.

Tube Pass - Anna

Roughly half of all graduates migrate to London for their first jobs. And oh I remember when I got my first London Oyster Card! That little blue plastic rectangle was a sign that I had truly arrived. I was a Londoner. Not a student who spends the odd weekend visiting friends – but a fully-fledged Londoner.

Let's put aside the fact that I would often go in the wrong direction on the tube, attempt to go in through the 'out' barriers and would have rather run a mile than negotiate the bus system. Even after two years I can still be seen doing my best tourist impersonation to ask a passer-by!

You might be seasoned Londoners, but if not – give yourself plenty of extra journey time, and don't be afraid to ask questions and make mistakes. Hey, if you get there early – you've just won yourself a coffee break! If not, employers are often sympathetic to us newbies, and also have a great understanding for delayed trains and broken-down tubes.

Sites like TFL (Transport for London) are fantastic and they have gone all smartphone savvy, so download their app. National rail have a fabulous app too. It's very handy to have in your pocket!

If you are going into part-time studying whilst working, you can apply for student Oyster cards in London. Money off? Now you can't sniff at that! And be sure to register your Oyster card online too – it allows you to see where your money is going and you can get the balance back if it is lost or stolen.

Transparent - Alexander

Sooner or later your colleagues will find out you have a Christian faith. And whether you like it or not, part of calling yourself a Christian means you will have to share that faith with those who do not know Jesus. This Way, Truth and Life stuff is a package deal.

Pray for those moments. Ask the Lord to give you boldness, sensitivity and joy as you talk about the most important thing ever known. Keep your eye on those who are more sympathetic to the faith. Jesus refers to 'good soil' when thinking about those who are in the process of getting to know God for themselves.

Do not be afraid of messing it up either. It's not about you. When the time comes just give an account for the hope you have in Jesus; have a go. Be honest about the stuff you know and those things you struggle with. Natural disasters will occur again and again in your life. Friends will ask you, "Why God does allow these things to happen?" Be transparent with how you see God and how you follow Jesus in the hardest times.

The Bible states that some people will respond with faith and start their own walk with their creator, whilst others will reject your faith and may even reject you in the process. Do not be afraid. The truth is that you carry the same message that turned the world upside down and saved you from darkness into light. If that message can bring light to millions of people across the world throughout history, then it can probably benefit some of those you work/drink/live/queue/eat with.

"Be excited for the adventure God has for you at work! You hear that university is the best time to witness, but God is with you everywhere you go. At work, you are with the same people, day in and day out, and they watch your life in stressful and easy situations. It is an incredible place of witness." - Jordan, 25

Umbrella - Alexander

Buy one. And don't just spend £1 at the local pound store, but get yourself one that survives in a breeze. Walking through your work's car park without an umbrella as the clouds explode above you is not ideal at 8.45am.

Vanilla - Alexander

When it's your turn to nip to the shops for some cake or ice creams, don't hold back. Even if it means you won't be able to afford your favourite bottle of red wine for the weekend (Apparently Jesus talked about 'denying yourself').

Get your work colleagues the best stuff. Go for the nice stuff on the shelf and don't always wait until it's your turn to get a round of treats in. Volunteer yourself to bring the goodies. People remember generosity and though we are saved by grace and not deeds, we are also called to bless those who don't always deserve it.

And find out what people prefer before buying a group of vegans a packet of Magnums!

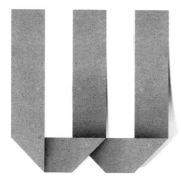

West Ham - Alexander

Lads, leave the football hooligan in you at the door. You will have to work alongside people from all different backgrounds every single day. So, get over yourself for the sake of friendship. By all means bring the banter in bucket loads, but be the first one to compliment another's team's effort. Be prepared to take an absolute slaughtering if your team gets smashed 6-1 by a lower side. Take it with a sense of humour. Let everyone around you know that sport is not your first priority.

And why not use the game as a pull to bring people together? If you happen to follow a team in the same division as one of your colleague's teams, take the time to go see the game together. Or why not arrange a big pub outing to see the international games? Men bond over shared experiences. It's a great opportunity to naturally introduce your non-Christian mates to other guys from church, allowing them to see other 'normal' guys who also follow Jesus. You never know where those conversations will lead...

Work Experience - Sarah-Jane

Where did you spend your Year 9 work experience? Do you still want to pursue that line of work? Probably not!

Work experience can feel like a waste of time – something we only do because school requires it or it looks good on a CV. But good work experience can be life-changing. It can provide a chance to see what a job looks like in practice, to test out whether it is an avenue you really want to go down. It can be a key time for making contacts that might later come in handy and could even lead to the offer of a paid job at the end of it.

Someone once said to me that I should think of every week's work experience as a week-long interview. It's sound advice. Ask yourself: Have I demonstrated that I am a valuable addition to the team and are they likely to remember me in 6-months' time when an opportunity opens up? And even if on day two you realise that the sector is really not for you, still work hard and recognise that the opportunity is a privilege, even if you are not being paid.

Be creative in getting work experience. Are there people in your church who would be happy to let you shadow them for a few days? Or perhaps there are distant relatives who could put you up for a short while in a city where there are more things on offer? I got very cheap lodging with a 93-year-old lady during one internship by working as her evening carer and doing all of household chores that she was no-longer able to do – the opportunities are there if you are willing to be creative!

"I had the impression that a degree would allow me to do whatever I wanted to straight away. I didn't realise how much time and effort it would take to build my career. I really wish that I had used my summer breaks to gain some work experience." – Caz, 30

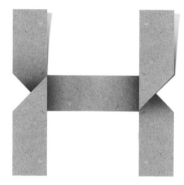

Xena Warrior Princess - Alexander

As your schedule gets totally revamped, you will find yourself taking up new hobbies. Many people use some of their first pay packets to buy a computer console and enjoy hours on end with their housemates beating each other up with axes in a virtual world. Morality aside, keep an eye out on how long you spend on the computer in your spare time.

Playing a console or updating Facebook to relax is totally fine and very effective, but make sure you are the one in control. Five hours every night on a computer is not OK. Make plans to do something else and stick to those plans.

If you find yourself becoming addicted to the virtual world, let someone in the church know about it. It's a very common problem and can be sorted by a few lifestyle adjustments.

Year Out - Sarah-Jane

If you didn't have a gap year before uni, you may well be considering one now. And even if you did, having another one might seem just as tempting!

A 'year out' can be a fantastic time – a time to explore new things, see new places and meet new people. A time to stretch the horizons of our own thinking by learning from cultures, neighbourhoods or streets different from our own. They can be times when we dare to do something unusual with God and push ourselves to serve him outside of our comfort zones. A time when we explore with God what we should do next and what steps would help us get there. You don't have to go to Africa, you can grow just as much in the charity down the road or the church you're a lifetime member of – it's the attitude that counts.

See, on the flip-side a 'year out' can also be thoroughly self-indulgent time, in which we postpone thinking about the realities of graduate life, clinging purposelessly to a student lifestyle we can't bear to let go of. A year in which we have low expectations of how God can use us, because we have shelved that one along with getting a job and being grown up. A year in which we tread water, making little progress only to face the big decisions just 365 days later.

If you are going to have a gap year – great, go for it, but make it count!

Youth - Alexander

A slight feeling of disdain for those still at university is not uncommon. Part of it comes from the desire to move away from the student culture and cement a place in the working world. However, don't pretend that you weren't immersed in their struggles, ambitions and issues less than a year ago.

Be prepared to help and mentor a student in Bible study or prayer. Make yourself available for those approaching their graduation and job searches. Also, don't feel that because you're now a proper adult that you can't go watch a gig at the student pubs. If something is good, it doesn't matter what culture it exists in.

Never be too proud to visit former lecturers to ask them how things are going and update them on your life. Stay on the radar because God may still use you in the lives that are seemingly drifting away from yours.

Zero - Alexander

We often dream of new starts and second chances. This point in the road is a fantastic time to change direction if that is what you feel is right to do. You might have studied art history but now don't feel any call to work in a gallery. That's OK – you're not confined to the degree that you studied. Don't think that because you spent three years of your life reading books on maths that you have to spend the next 50 years doing the same thing. New discoveries are waiting for us all every day. Don't be afraid to change your mind, even if it means surprising your parents, friends and church leaders.

We bring nothing into this world and we can take nothing out of it...not even our degrees! Make decisions based on the fact that the creator of all things has adopted you through the sacrifice of his son, Jesus. It really does put things into perspective. Don't beat yourself up if you think you've 'wasted' your degree. Nothing is wasted in God's currency and you will have picked up tons of skills that will transfer to a new arena.

For every graduate, this is a great time to pause and reflect. Ask yourself, 'What things about my time at uni am I really proud of? What has God been teaching me and how can I use these lessons in this next chapter?' And think about the flip-side too: 'What about my time at uni am I not so proud of? What things do I want to draw a line in the sand over and change in the year ahead?'

What are you going to dream with God for in this next phase?

Lord Jesus...

Thank you for bringing me to this point,
For being with me during the highs and lows of my time at uni,
For blessing me with the awesome privilege of doing a degree,
For the amazing people I've met and all the lessons learnt along the way.

I'm sorry for the times when I've not trusted you enough,
For the times when I've freaked out about where I'm going next,
For the times when I've become so blinkered by my own wants,
That I've not seen the needs of those around me.

Jesus, for all of the things I have lined up for next year,
Would you show me how to use them to glorify you, not me,
For all of the things that are still unknown, Lord, you know my needs;
Help me to make wise choices and to trust that you do provide.

This new chapter of life is going to take some getting used to,
Holy Spirit, would you be close to me as I go,
Would you nudge me to see the kingdom opportunities in my everyday,
So that my work, rest and play may bring you praise.

Amen.

About LICC

The London Institute for Contemporary Christianity (LICC) was founded in 1982 by the Revd Dr John R W Stott, who saw an urgent need to enable Christians and their churches to connect the living word of the living God to the issues they face in a rapidly changing world.

Today our work holds that same vision with two main aims:

+ To envision and equip 'ordinary' Christians for their 'frontlines' in the world.

+ To enable local church communities to become whole-life disciple-making communities – and to stay that way.

How We Work

LICC has three main centres that work together to make whole-life discipleship central and unavoidable in the UK church:

+ Bible & Culture: From beginning to end, Scripture tells of God's redemptive purposes not only for the church but for all creation, including our own role in that great plan. So all of our work is grounded in Scripture, listening to both the Word and the world to understand and respond to the challenges and opportunities of contemporary life.

+ Imagine Project: Since 2003 the Imagine Projects has explored Jesus post resurrection command, "Make disciples" and together with local churches, we've discovered some fresh, simple ways of doing church which integrates concern for neighbourhood and overseas mission, with the opportunities and challenges people have out on their daily frontlines.

+ WorkForum: For many Christians the workplace is the frontline where they spend most time and the most time with people who don't know Jesus. We've been pioneers in workplace ministry for over 20 years and the WorkForum seeks to support and equip people to be faithful, fruitful employees and servants of the King.

Other resources available from LICC include:

TOOLBOX   Five days engaging with the Bible and
                                contemporary culture. Great for recent graduates.

PRAYERWORKS   Free 40-day e-prayer journeys designed to help
                                you to pray for your work.

THE GREAT DIVIDE   A short, compelling essay exploring the effect of
                                the sacred-secular divide on Christian mission and
                                living and suggesting what we can do about it.

THANK GOD IT'S MONDAY   A fun, fast-paced and highly practical book helping
                                us see how our work life, as well as our weekend
                                life, can be lived fruitfully for God.

LIFE ON THE FRONTLINE   A 'brilliantly accessible' 6 session DVD-based
                                course to help you and your small group live
                                fruitfully in the daily places of life and work.

TRANSITION   A booklet helping students and graduates think
                                about life after uni dealing with unemployment,
                                power and humility and many other topics.

WORD FOR THE WEEK   A punchy weekly email delivered on a Monday
                                earthing Scripture in real-life contexts.

CONNECTING WITH CULTURE   A weekly email delivered on a Friday reflecting on
                                different aspects of contemporary culture from a
                                biblical perspective.

LIBRARY OF FREE RESOURCES   Use our excellent web resources and clips by
                                visiting www.licc.org.uk/resources

The London Institute for
Contemporary Christianity

For more information on our resources and the work
of LICC, contact us at:
LICC
St Peter's
Vere Street
London
W1G 0DQ
0207 399 9555 | mail@licc.org.uk | www.licc.org.uk

About Fusion

The ministry of Fusion emerged in 1997 as a response to a shared vision across the body of Christ to address the challenges of a changing student world. We believe God's passion is for a dynamic student movement, one that will see universities and colleges won for Christ.

Future Dreams

We are about connecting student to church and church to student. Not just one or two but serving thousands of churches in reaching and discipling millions of students. We are convinced that local church needs to be at the heart of student mission and students at the heart of local church.

What We're Doing Today

Fusion is fuelling the fires of a national student movement through our three purposes:

+ Equipping Students: Inspiring evangelism, resourcing discipleship and preparing new students for university

+ Serving Churches: Connecting students to church, catalysing mission and strengthening church-based student work

+ Developing Student Workers: Training, resourcing and encouraging all those in student ministry

How Are We Doing It?

Fusion's values under pin all that we do and outline how the mission of Fusion is outworked. We are committed to being:

Biblical, Relational, Missional, Catalytic and Inclusive.

Fusion works in partnership at all levels of our organisation. At present we serve in conjunction with around 30 organisations, denominations and church streams. We look to be inclusive and labour alongside those who wish to see a significant move of God in the universities of the UK.

We invite you to partner with us in bringing God's love to the universities, to see a generation respond to Jesus.

Other resources available from Fusion include:

Studentscape	A discipleship resource for new students.
The Student Alphabet	An A-Z for starting Uni.
The Student Linkup Trainer Pack	Everything you need to prepare school leavers for uni.
The Student Linkup Starting Uni Pack	The must have resource for every new student
University: The Big Challenge	360° Preparation for student life
www.studentlinkup.org	Find and connect to a new church at uni.
Fuse magazine	News, stories and updates from students and local churches around the country and a directory of churches that welcome and support students.

To find out more please visit www.fusion.uk.com/resources

For more information on our resources and the work of Fusion contact us at:

Fusion UK

Unit 18

The Office Village

North Road

Loughborough

LE11 1QJ

01509 268 505 | hello@fusion.uk.com | www.fusion.uk.com